The Clan of
One-Breasted Women

The Clan of
One-Breasted Women

TERRY TEMPEST
WILLIAMS

PENGUIN BOOKS — GREEN IDEAS

PENGUIN BOOKS

UK | USA | Canada | Ireland | Australia
India | New Zealand | South Africa

Penguin Books is part of the Penguin Random House group of companies
whose addresses can be found at global.penguinrandomhouse.com.

'The Clan of One-Breasted Women' first published in *Refuge*, 1991
'Paper, Rock, Scissors' and 'A Totemic Act'
first published in *Erosion: Essays of Undoing*, 2019
Prelude to 'The Erotic Landscape' from *Leap*, 2000
'The Erotic Landscape' from *RED: Passion and Patience in the Desert*, 1998,
first appeared in *Northern Lights* magazine.
'Ground Truthing' and 'Engagement' first published by *Orion* Magazine
This selection published in Penguin Books 2021

001

Set in 11.5/14pt Dante MT Std
Typeset by Jouve (UK), Milton Keynes
Printed and bound in Great Britain by Clays Ltd, Elcograf S.p.A.

The authorized representative in the EEA is Penguin Random House Ireland,
Morrison Chambers, 32 Nassau Street, Dublin D02 YH68

A CIP catalogue record for this book is available from the British Library

ISBN: 978-0-241-51458-0

www.greenpenguin.co.uk

Contents

The Clan of One-Breasted Women

I belong to a Clan of One-Breasted Women. My mother, my grandmothers, and six aunts have all had mastectomies. Seven are dead. The two who survive have just completed rounds of chemotherapy and radiation.

I've had my own problems: two biopsies for breast cancer and a small tumor between my ribs diagnosed as a 'borderline malignancy.'

This is my family history.

Most statistics tell us breast cancer is genetic, hereditary, with rising percentages attached to fatty diets, childlessness, or becoming pregnant after thirty. What they don't say is living in Utah may be the greatest hazard of all.

We are a Mormon family with roots in Utah since 1847. The 'word of wisdom' in my family aligned us with good foods – no coffee, no tea, tobacco, or alcohol. For the most part, our women were finished having their babies by the time they were thirty. And only one faced breast cancer prior to 1960.

Traditionally, as a group of people, Mormons have a low rate of cancer.

Is our family a cultural anomaly? The truth is, we didn't think about it. Those who did, usually the men, simply said, 'bad genes.' The women's attitude was stoic. Cancer was part of life. On February 16, 1971, the eve of my mother's surgery, I accidently picked up the telephone and overheard her ask my grandmother what she could expect.

'Diane, it is one of the most spiritual experiences you will ever encounter.'

I quietly put down the receiver.

Two days later, my father took my brothers and me to the hospital to visit her. She met us in the lobby in a wheelchair. No bandages were visible. I'll never forget her radiance, the way she held herself in a purple velvet robe, and how she gathered us around her.

'Children, I am fine. I want you to know I felt the arms of God around me.'

We believed her. My father cried. Our mother, his wife, was thirty-eight years old.

A little over a year after Mother's death, Dad and I were having dinner together. He had just returned from St. George, where the Tempest Company was completing the gas lines that would service southern Utah. He spoke of his love for the country, the sandstoned landscape, bare-boned and beautiful. He had just finished hiking the Kolob trail in Zion National Park. We got caught up in reminiscing, recalling with fondness our walk up Angel's Landing on his fiftieth birthday and the years our family had vacationed there.

Over dessert, I shared a recurring dream of mine. I told my father that for years, as long as I could remember, I saw this flash of light in the night in the desert – that this image had so permeated my being that I could not venture south without seeing it again, on the horizon, illuminating buttes and mesas.

'You did see it,' he said.

'Saw what?'

'The bomb. The cloud. We were driving home from Riverside, California. You were sitting on Diane's lap. She was pregnant. In fact, I remember the day, September 7, 1957. We had just gotten out of the Service. We were driving north, past Las Vegas. It was an hour or so before dawn, when this explosion went off. We not only heard it, but felt it. I thought the oil tanker in front of us had blown up. We pulled over and suddenly, rising from the desert floor, we saw it, clearly, this golden-stemmed cloud, the mushroom. The sky seemed to vibrate with an eerie pink glow. Within a few minutes, a light ash was raining on the car.'

I stared at my father.

'I thought you knew that,' he said. 'It was a common occurrence in the fifties.'

It was at this moment that I realized the deceit I had been living under. Children growing up in the American Southwest, drinking contaminated milk from contaminated cows, even from the contaminated breasts of their mothers, my mother – members, years later, of the Clan of One-Breasted Women.

It is a well-known story in the Desert West, 'The Day We Bombed Utah,' or more accurately, the years we bombed Utah: above ground atomic testing in Nevada took place from January 27, 1951 through July 11, 1962. Not only were the winds blowing north covering 'low-use segments of the population' with fallout and leaving sheep dead in their tracks, but the climate was right. The United States of the 1950s was red, white, and blue. The Korean War was raging. McCarthyism was rampant. Ike was it, and the cold war was hot. If you were against nuclear testing, you were for a communist regime.

Much has been written about this 'American nuclear tragedy.' Public health was secondary to national security. The Atomic Energy Commissioner, Thomas Murray, said, 'Gentlemen, we must not let anything interfere with this series of tests, nothing.'

Again and again, the American public was told by

its government, in spite of burns, blisters, and nausea, 'It has been found that the tests may be conducted with adequate assurance of safety under conditions prevailing at the bombing reservations.' Assuaging public fears was simply a matter of public relations. 'Your best action,' an Atomic Energy Commission booklet read, 'is not to be worried about fallout.' A news release typical of the times stated, 'We find no basis for concluding that harm to any individual has resulted from radioactive fallout.'

On August 30, 1979, during Jimmy Carter's presidency, a suit was filed, *Irene Allen v. The United States of America*. Mrs Allen's case was the first on an alphabetical list of twenty-four test cases, representative of nearly twelve hundred plaintiffs seeking compensation from the United States government for cancers caused by nuclear testing in Nevada.

Irene Allen lived in Hurricane, Utah. She was the mother of five children and had been widowed twice. Her first husband, with their two oldest boys, had watched the tests from the roof of the local high school. He died of leukemia in 1956. Her second husband died of pancreatic cancer in 1978.

In a town meeting conducted by Utah Senator Orrin Hatch, shortly before the suit was filed, Mrs Allen said, 'I am not blaming the government, I want you to know that, Senator Hatch. But I thought if my testimony could help in any way so this wouldn't happen again to any of the generations coming up after us . . . I am happy to be here this day to bear testimony of this.'

God-fearing people. This is just one story in an anthology of thousands.

On May 10, 1984, Judge Bruce S. Jenkins handed down his opinion. Ten of the plaintiffs were awarded damages. It was the first time a federal court had determined that nuclear tests had been the cause of cancers. For the remaining fourteen test cases, the proof of causation was not sufficient. In spite of the split decision, it was considered a landmark ruling. It was not to remain so for long.

In April 1987, the Tenth Circuit Court of Appeals overturned Judge Jenkins's ruling on the ground that the United States was protected from suit by the legal doctrine of sovereign immunity, a centuries-old idea from England in the days of absolute monarchs.

In January 1988, the Supreme Court refused to review the Appeals Court decision. To our court system it does not matter whether the United States government was irresponsible, whether it lied to its citizens, or even that citizens died from the fallout of nuclear testing. What matters is that our government is immune: 'The King can do no wrong.'

In Mormon culture, authority is respected, obedience

is revered, and independent thinking is not. I was taught as a young girl not to 'make waves' or 'rock the boat.'

'Just let it go,' Mother would say. 'You know how you feel, that's what counts.'

For many years, I have done just that – listened, observed, and quietly formed my own opinions, in a culture that rarely asks questions because it has all the answers. But one by one, I have watched the women in my family die common, heroic deaths. We sat in waiting rooms hoping for good news, but always receiving the bad. I cared for them, bathed their scarred bodies, and kept their secrets. I watched beautiful women become bald as Cytoxan, cisplatin, and Adriamycin were injected into their veins. I held their foreheads as they vomited green-black bile, and I shot them with morphine when the pain became inhuman. In the end, I witnessed their last peaceful breaths, becoming a midwife to the rebirth of their souls.

The price of obedience has become too high.

The fear and inability to question authority that ultimately killed rural communities in Utah during atmospheric testing of atomic weapons is the same fear I saw in my mother's body. Sheep. Dead sheep. The evidence is buried.

I cannot prove that my mother, Diane Dixon Tempest, or my grandmothers, Lettie Romney Dixon

7

and Kathryn Blackett Tempest, along with my aunts developed cancer from nuclear fallout in Utah. But I can't prove they didn't.

My father's memory was correct. The September blast we drove through in 1957 was part of Operation Plumbbob, one of the most intensive series of bomb tests to be initiated. The flash of light in the night in the desert, which I had always thought was a dream, developed into a family nightmare. It took fourteen years, from 1957 to 1971, for cancer to manifest in my mother – the same time, Howard L. Andrews, an authority in radioactive fallout at the National Institutes of Health, says radiation cancer requires to become evident. The more I learn about what it means to be a 'downwinder,' the more questions I drown in.

What I do know, however, is that as a Mormon woman of the fifth generation of Latter-day Saints, I must question everything, even if it means losing my faith, even if it means becoming a member of a border tribe among my own people. Tolerating blind obedience in the name of patriotism or religion ultimately takes our lives.

When the Atomic Energy Commission described the country north of the Nevada Test Site as 'virtually uninhabited desert terrain,' my family and the birds at Great Salt Lake were some of the 'virtual uninhabitants.'

★

One night, I dreamed women from all over the world circled a blazing fire in the desert. They spoke of change, how they hold the moon in their bellies and wax and wane with its phases. They mocked the presumption of even-tempered beings and made promises that they would never fear the witch inside themselves. The women danced wildly as sparks broke away from the flames and entered the night sky as stars.

And they sang a song given to them by Shoshone grandmothers:

Ah ne nah, nah	Consider the rabbits
nin nah nah –	How gently they walk on the earth –
ah ne nah, nah	Consider the rabbits
nin nah nah –	How gently they walk on the earth –
Nyaga mutzi	We remember them
oh ne nay –	We can walk gently also –
Nyaga mutzi	We remember them
oh ne nay –	We can walk gently also –

The women danced and drummed and sang for weeks, preparing themselves for what was to come. They would reclaim the desert for the sake of their children, for the sake of the land.

A few miles downwind from the fire circle, bombs were being tested. Rabbits felt the tremors. Their soft leather pads on paws and feet recognized the shaking sands, while the roots of mesquite and sage were smoldering. Rocks were hot from the inside out and dust devils hummed unnaturally. And each time there was another nuclear test, ravens watched the desert heave. Stretch marks appeared. The land was losing its muscle.

The women couldn't bear it any longer. They were mothers. They had suffered labor pains but always under the promise of birth. The red hot pains beneath the desert promised death only, as each bomb became a stillborn. A contract had been made and broken between human beings and the land. A new contract was being drawn by the women, who understood the fate of the earth as their own.

Under the cover of darkness, ten women slipped under a barbed-wire fence and entered the contaminated country. They were trespassing. They walked toward the town of Mercury, in moonlight, taking their cues from coyote, kit fox, antelope squirrel, and quail. They moved quietly and deliberately through the maze of Joshua trees. When a hint of daylight appeared they rested, drinking tea and sharing their rations of food. The women closed their eyes. The time had come to protest with the heart, that to deny one's genealogy with the earth was to commit treason against one's soul.

At dawn, the women draped themselves in mylar,

wrapping long streamers of silver plastic around their arms to blow in the breeze. They wore clear masks, that became the faces of humanity. And when they arrived at the edge of Mercury, they carried all the butterflies of a summer day in their wombs. They paused to allow their courage to settle.

The town that forbids pregnant women and children to enter because of radiation risks was asleep. The women moved through the streets as winged messengers, twirling around each other in slow motion, peeking inside homes and watching the easy sleep of men and women. They were astonished by such stillness and periodically would utter a shrill note or low cry just to verify life.

The residents finally awoke to these strange apparitions. Some simply stared. Others called authorities, and in time, the women were apprehended by wary soldiers dressed in desert fatigues. They were taken to a white, square building on the other edge of Mercury. When asked who they were and why they were there, the women replied, 'We are mothers and we have come to reclaim the desert for our children.'

The soldiers arrested them. As the ten women were blindfolded and handcuffed, they began singing:

> *You can't forbid us everything*
> *You can't forbid us to think –*

You can't forbid our tears to flow
And you can't stop the songs that we sing.

The women continued to sing louder and louder, until they heard the voices of their sisters moving across the mesa:

Ah ne nah, nah
nin nah nah –
Ah ne nah, nah
nin nah nah –
Nyaga mutzi
oh ne nay –
Nyaga mutzi
oh ne nay –

'Call for reinforcements,' one soldier said.

'We have,' interrupted one woman, 'we have – and you have no idea of our numbers.'

I crossed the line at the Nevada Test Site and was arrested with nine other Utahns for trespassing on military lands. They are still conducting nuclear tests in the desert. Ours was an act of civil disobedience. But as I walked towards the town of Mercury, it was more than a gesture of peace. It was a gesture on behalf of the Clan of One-Breasted Women.

As one officer cinched the handcuffs around my wrists, another frisked my body. She found a pen and a pad of paper tucked inside my left boot.

'And these?' she asked sternly.

'Weapons,' I replied.

Our eyes met. I smiled. She pulled the leg of my trousers back over my boot.

'Step forward, please,' she said as she took my arm.

We were booked under an afternoon sun and bused to Tonopah, Nevada. It was a two-hour ride. This was familiar country. The Joshua trees standing their ground had been named by my ancestors, who believed they looked like prophets pointing west to the Promised Land. These were the same trees that bloomed each spring, flowers appearing like white flames in the Mojave. And I recalled a full moon in May, when Mother and I had walked among them, flushing out mourning doves and owls.

The bus stopped short of town. We were released.

The officials thought it was a cruel joke to leave us stranded in the desert with no way to get home. What they didn't realize was that we were home, soul-centered and strong, women who recognized the sweet smell of sage as fuel for our spirits.

1991

Paper, Rock, Scissors

The Wilderness Act, 1964–2014
With Brooke Williams

Paper. Rock. Scissors. For some, wilderness is a game to win or lose. Paper covers rock. Rock crushes scissors. Scissors cut paper bills to shreds. For others, however, wilderness is a place, a state of being where open spaces open minds. In the stillness of a red rock canyon, we hear what has been lost to us – windsong, birdsong, the hymns of rivers resounding. Coyotes call up the moon. We see what has been obscured – sandstone sculpted through time, a night sky of stars. No longer numb, we feel ourselves alive, awakened.

We make our choices and calculations in the form of gestures: an open hand; a fist; fingers moving up and down to cut. Wilderness as a game is played at our own peril. 'One, two, three, go –' When both players choose the same gesture, the game is tied.

Our hands are tied today by Washington's special interests. Big oil translates to big profits. The development of public lands by the extractive industry is money made and delivered into the private coffers of corporations. The revenues from oil and gas, tar sands, and coal will continue to build the yellow-cake roads paving the way to uranium mines, illuminating what we know to be true: our economy is more important than ecology; conservation is mocked by capitalism; what we consume matters more than what we contemplate. When it comes to wilderness, 'the open space of democracy' drowns in the wake of greed.

Intimidation is key. The political terrorism of the Far Right inspires the militias, who back the ranchers, who refuse to pay what they owe to the American people for grazing on public lands. Federal agencies like the Bureau of Land Management care more about keeping the peace than protecting the public commons.

Paper. Rock. Scissors. The stakes could not be higher.

Paper

The Wilderness Act of 1964 was conceived as an open hand, a gesture of peace on behalf of wildlands, a protection and a promise that what is wild will remain wild and free. On this piece of paper, the Wilderness Act brought the eloquence of the land into the elegance of language. On this piece of paper, these words stand as a definition of wilderness:

A wilderness, in contrast with those areas where man
and his own works dominate the landscape, is hereby
recognized as an area where the earth and its community of life are untrammeled by man, where man
himself is a visitor who does not remain . . . an area of
undeveloped Federal land retaining its primeval
character and influence . . . protected and managed
so as to preserve its natural conditions and which . . .
appears to have been affected primarily by the forces
of nature, with the imprint of man's work substan-
tially unnoticeable; has outstanding opportunities for
solitude or a primitive and unconfined type of recreation; has at least five thousand acres of land or is of
sufficient size . . . and may also contain ecological,
geological, or other features of scientific, educational,
scenic, or historical value.

By honoring wilderness, we honor beauty. Beauty
is not peripheral, but at the core of what sustains us.
Awe and wonder ignite our imagination. We are
inspired. We witness the magnificent and miraculous nature of creation. We are humbled. Wilderness
becomes soul-settling; a homecoming; a reminder of
what we have forgotten – that where there is harmony
there is wholeness. The world is interconnected and
interrelated. Wild nature is not only to be protected,
but celebrated.

On September 3, 2014, the Wilderness Act celebrated its fiftieth anniversary. How has our thinking about wilderness evolved in these five decades?

The reasoning behind the Wilderness Act has not changed, but intensified. It is doubtful that the act's authors could have foreseen the levels of 'increasing population, accompanied by expanding settlement and growing mechanization' that now threaten to move wild lands from the place of protection to the place of extinction. Climate change was a concept unknown to them, climate crisis unthinkable. Now these words are being used to redefine why wilderness matters in the twenty-first century.

As the Earth heats up, wilderness offers a cooling of the senses, a storing of the waters, and a bank of biodiversity where carbon is held, not spent. Wilderness becomes an insurance policy against ecological disasters caused by desertification, acidification, and mindless development that also leaves the land bare of beauty and vulnerable. Erosion becomes the story; dust, the narrative; and a scorched stratigraphy in the American Southwest beyond drought that creates a desolation unimaginable except in stories of apocalypse.

The Wilderness Act of 1964 became an act of restraint in 2014. The Wilderness Act, fifty years after its creation, remains an act of wisdom.

Did Howard Zahniser and Olaus Murie, the chief

architects of the Wilderness Act, consciously create a definition for wilderness that would project us into the future?

The importance of wildness keeps expanding as our need for wilderness increases. 'Scenic wilderness' helps us appreciate nature's grandeur. Wilderness that is ecologically and geologically diverse must now be folded into our society, which is equally diverse, allowing us to see the natural world as a web of fascinating and complex interconnected systems. And now, the idea of solitude in wilderness becomes the seminal gift at a time when we are on the verge of letting the noise of our own technologies drown out the sound of life itself.

The Wilderness Act of 1964 has not changed, we have. We read the landscape of our lives differently. Our connection to the world is virtual, not real. An apple is not just a fruit but a computer. A mouse is not simply a rodent but a controlling mechanism for a cursor. We have moved ourselves from the outdoors to the indoors. Nature is no longer a force but a source of images for our screensavers. We sit. We stare. We text on our iPhones and type on our keyboards, and await an immediate response. Patience is an endangered species. Intimacy is a threatened landscape.

Wilderness brings us back home to our bodies. We remember what it means to be challenged physically and stretched emotionally. We watch the weather and

wonder if danger is near. It thunders. Lightning strikes.
It rains. We are cold. We keep going in the midst of
adverse conditions. The rain stops. We dry as the land
dries. A rainbow arches over the horizon. In wilderness, time is not measured in money but in miles, in
the hours spent walking on a trail. The wealth of a day
in wildness is measured in increments of awe.

The outer wilderness mirrors our inner wilderness.
Our adventurous nature is intrinsically tied to wild
nature. A freedom of spirit depends on big, wide open
spaces, the same spaces that gave birth to our nation
and were home already to hundreds of other nations
of indigenous people for generations. If we destroy
what is outside us, we will destroy what is inside us.
Something precious and original is lost. The 'home of
the brave and the land of the free' disappears. Mad-
ness fills the void. Wilderness is a stay against insanity.
The Wilderness Act of 1964 is a prescription. 'We need
the tonic of the wilderness' – Thoreau knew this two
centuries ago.

Do we?

Rock

The Wilderness Act originally covered rock and ice:
nine million acres were to be protected, from the

mountains in the Sierra Nevada to the Bridger-Teton National Forest to the Boundary Waters of Minnesota. The Wilderness Act signed into law on September 3, 1964, by President Lyndon B. Johnson became an act of generosity, an honoring of a communal wealth to be held in a public trust. These wildlands are not owned by a single species but shared with a community of species, so all might flourish. To designate wilderness is to honor the natural order of a place free from the hands of humans. Yet, the Wilderness Act is not without its irony. It was through human hands that this law came into being. And it will be through human hands that wilderness will continue.

Wilderness designation is 'in the highest tradition of our heritage as conservators as well as users of America's bountiful natural endowments,' said President Johnson. 'The wilderness bill preserves for our posterity, for all time to come, 9 million acres of this vast continent in their original and unchanging beauty and wonder . . . Americans have wisely and have courageously kept a faithful trust to the conservation of our natural resources and beauty.'

Earth First! raised the clenched fist that defined the wilderness movement in the 1970s. 'The idea of wilderness needs no defense, it only needs defenders,' wrote Edward Abbey. And defenders we have. More than fifty years later, over 110 million acres have been added to the list, honored and protected by designation with more than 800 wilderness areas secured in all fifty states. And wilderness bills in Utah, New Mexico, and Montana are slow but ongoing.

Wilderness is a place where we experience the quiet and sometimes violent unfolding of nature, where the natural processes of life are sustained and supported. It is where we feel the rightness of relationships, where we sense our true place, a part of, not apart from, the forces of life. Wilderness is harmony revisited with adaptations unexpected and surprising like the first shining organisms that shimmered toward life, emerging from that steamy primordial swamp. And just like every other creature, we are selected for and selected against. Wilderness returns us to this one simple fact: we are animals. Unlike the world of humans, who trade on greed, scarcity, and selfishness, nature functions on frugality, abundance, and altruism. Nothing wasted. Yes, there is a brutality to the wild, but there is also resiliency in the renewal of each day.

Wilderness is akin to love, flush with chemical reactions hormonal and pheromonal, a firing of synapses in our brain that is integral to our survival. We are propelled by the currents of connection. Isolation is quelled. Fear is replaced by awe. We recognize wildness as creativity in the extreme. We are not in control. We surrender to solitude. We sit on the edge of a canyon looking out – and in the marvel of a moment far beyond ourselves, we inhale, exhale, relax, and swoon.

Scissors

Scissors are a singular object made plural through language: a pair of scissors is one tool where two blades of metal are pivoted so the sharpened edges slide against each other in a common purpose. They can cut, slice, stab, or wound depending on whose hand directs them. To leave a pair of scissors open is to flirt with superstition that a fight will ensue. To open and close scissors mindlessly is to call in bad luck.

But in the game of paper, rock, scissors, the rock beats scissors every time. The clenched fist has supremacy over the first two fingers extended and touching. The rock of resistance can crush the political scissors of bureaucracy that threaten to destroy the paper bills that protect wilderness, even the Wilderness Act itself, so eloquently drafted by Howard Zahniser with friends on the porch of the Murie cabin in Moose, Wyoming.

These pragmatic visionaries who believed as Thoreau did that 'wildness is the preservation of the world,' made a commitment to the future. They saw wilderness not as the haunt of the elite, but the domain of everyone, regardless of race, class, or gender. Wildness is central to the cause of humanity. They built a foundation from which to care, a platform where humility embraced an intelligence of the wild. Nancy Newhall wrote in *This Is the American Earth*: 'Wilderness holds the answers to more questions then we yet know how to ask.'

They passed this rock on to us as we now pass it on to the next generation, who will pass it on to the one that follows them with the long-standing view that wild lands and wild lives deserve our respect. Wilderness protection is a generational embrace. This rock has been rolling through the halls of Washington for five decades with its own solid momentum. Conservation is a prayer and a practice for the life that is to come.

Wilderness is not a game. We must change the rules of engagement. Paper can be used for a map. A rock keeps the map in place. And the scissors can be retired. We have cut enough wilderness out of the heart of the American landscape. The Chinese believe that if you give a pair of scissors to someone you cut ties with them. We need to restore our ties to wild nature. It is time to draw up a new map of wilderness that is more inclusive, not just of our species, and with a broader understanding that we are living in a time of climate confirmation: the Earth is heating up.

The remaining wild places can guide us and protect us as we move toward an uncertain and evolving future.

Evolution as a Strategy

There is revolution, an evolution, occurring on our public lands. There are those who want to sell them, abuse them, and write them off as a collective take-over of our individual rights and freedoms by the federal government. The Bundy standoff in 2016 at Malheur National Wildlife Refuge showed us where this leads. There are others who see our public lands as a public trust in the name of future generations and the life that is to come – be it a child or a wolf pup or a canyon wren singing in the desert.

This revolution is taking place primarily in the American West, where it can be viewed as a battlefield or as a turning point in how we choose to live. Revolution inspires evolution, and we see the fear it is awakening in the bloodshot eyes of angry white men – star-spangled Americans who feel their power and influence slipping away. Blinded by their own sense of privilege, they fail to see how their patriarchal foundation built on guns, gas, and American exceptionalism is the very obstacle to the future they say they are fighting to protect. Their ideological cornerstone is crumbling.

How many shenanigans must we endure alongside the posturing, the posing, and the polemics that precede the actual destruction ensuing from their fear of a changing world. The 'sagebrush rebels' who reincarnate each decade will bulldoze another road in the wilderness to show the wilderness has been tamed. Men with loaded guns wait and watch. Militias preparing for war stand guard. And now we have another cry of hysteria: 'Build that Wall!' It is a wall against not only immigrants and asylum seekers, but wildlife and butterfly sanctuaries and corridors. If wilderness teaches us anything, it is that borders need to be fluid, not fixed.

Meanwhile, America's public lands, our national parks and monuments, have become places of pilgrimage, landscapes loved and cherished, most of them bordered by wilderness. Gateway communities to our parks are thriving. And the outdoor industry is a burgeoning business, one that may be contributing to the risk of loving these lands to death as more and more people seek solace in nature. Reservation systems at our parks and wilderness areas are becoming more common, despite the resistance. The revolution is coming; it just might not be what the old guard is planning.

Here is a prediction: the decade ahead will be one of the most crucial breakdown or breakthrough moments in the history of our species.

It is not a game of paper, rock, or scissors.

Wilderness offers us a template to an enlightened citizenship. Instead of only caring for ourselves, we are invited to care for species other than our own. We are encouraged to look to the roots of things. 'Care' is tied to the German root word *chara*, which means 'to grieve' or 'to lament.' To care about wilderness is to grieve over what we have lost. To care about wilderness is to fall back in love with the world and lament how lost we are, and how lonely we have become. We are losing our minds. It is time to return to our senses and recognize that the bedrock of our sanity lies in every square inch of wilderness that remains.

Designating wilderness in the twenty-first century must include designating wider access for diverse communities to engage in wild nature. Issues of racial diversity, equity, and engagement must be woven into the fabric of protecting wildlands, while at the same time we must understand that these lands hold not only the natural histories of plants and animals, but human histories, varied and oftentimes violent histories. The complexity of these landscapes must be named and honored, not hidden as it has been in the past, with the erasure of Native Peoples from our national parks. We can begin to see wilderness in broader terms, a place where ecological health is sustained and environmental justice is maintained for all species.

For marginalized communities to feel supported in wilderness, not alienated from it or at risk, the separation narratives of a wilderness without people must cease, so that our survival and the survival of the planet can be woven together into a story of wholeness and planetary health.

Clean water and clean air are human rights. By its very nature, wilderness safeguards an intersectionality of concerns. Wildlands that frame our communities contribute to sustainable economies through recreation and tourism. Wilderness fosters a peace of mind that affects our physical and mental health. Forests are a vital source of carbon sequestration. These gifts are not just for us, but are meant to be extended beyond ourselves, beyond our own time.

The biologist E. O. Wilson advocates protecting the planet's remaining biodiversity in his book *Half-Earth*. He maintains 'that the situation facing us is too large to be solved piecemeal and a solution commensurate with the magnitude of the problem is needed: dedicate fully half the surface of the Earth to nature.' Much of that open space will be wilderness.

Wilderness is a necessity, not a luxury. Our experiences with the wild strengthen us and provide us with uncommon insights capable of moving us toward an evolutionary grace that enables us to be in relationship with all beings.

We have been with students on a sandstone bluff looking west across Utah's Sweetwater Reef, a proposed wilderness area near Canyonlands, surrounded by a dense quiet, watching. They are not looking for something in particular, not places for cows to graze or junipers to be bulldozed, or trying to see how many gallons of oil might be pooled and plotted for a cross-country pipeline. They are simply looking out to where the Earth curves – beyond a symphony of time.

'Wildness is evolution,' says Michael Soule. As a conservation biologist, he sees wilderness as the place where all elements are working in concert as a natural system that has one goal: passing life on to the future. As humans, we not only evolved in wilderness, but we continue to evolve in wilderness. Wilderness ensures possibilities. Saving wilderness is about saving ourselves, as well as protecting the evolutionary integrity of all other life forms on the planet. An open hand and a clenched fist will be required, along with a generous heart that dares to feel enough to grieve and lament what we are watching disappear and try to slow down the destruction we have set in motion.

Evolution is about adapting to changing conditions. But climate changes are occurring faster than we can biologically evolve or adapt. Because we humans have so quickly modified the planet's ability to support life, we must call on different forms of evolutionary adaptations, conscious and deliberate, diverging away from anything we've yet been able to perceive. What if at the individual level, wildness takes the form of imagination? Imagination leads us to creative acts. Wilderness in the twenty-first century is not a site of nostalgia for what once was, but rather the seedbed of creativity for what we have yet to imagine.

2019

A Totemic Act

The Endangered Species Act

The Endangered Species Act celebrated its fortieth birthday on Saturday, December 28, 2013. As the year drew to a close, it's safe to say, no one reported the good news of saving a wee wildflower or included it on any year-end list of big moments in Utah. A small wildflower that grows in the Kaibab Formation in Washington County, known as a Gierisch mallow (*Sphaeralcea gierischii*), was finally granted protection under the federal Endangered Species Act. Only eighteen populations or communities of these rare plants, approximately five thousand to eight thousand individuals, remain on Earth. This vibrant orange crepe-petaled flower with yellow stamens can be seen squeezed between Interstate 15 and the Virgin River.

Some may say, 'So what?' But if we look at the success story behind the 1973 Endangered Species Act, and where wild creatures stand today, we may be impressed by what a single law with vision can do. Species who are facing decreasing numbers as the result of various factors have legal protection under this prescient act. Birds like the bald eagle, peregrine falcon, and California condor were on the path to extinction in the 1960s because of such pesticides as DDT. Today, the bald eagle population is vulnerable but stable; same with the peregrines. Both have been taken off the endangered species list.

The California condor was on the brink of extinction in 1987, with only twenty-two individuals left in the wild. Now, still 'critically endangered,' it has been successfully introduced in the Grand Canyon and Zion National Park through a captive breeding program. When their immense wings, spanning eleven feet, cross over you, casting their shadow as they soar effortlessly across the chasm at the South Rim, you feel the temperature drop. These are regal birds of prey that harken back to the Pleistocene. Each time I hold a condor in my binoculars, I am reminded of what care has been taken to keep their ancient spirits alive. It is reported that close to five hundred California condors are now living in the wild or captivity. From Baja California to Big Sur to the mountains of Ojai to the red rock desert canyons, they continue to animate the American landscape thanks to legal protection.

Since 2018, Senator John Barrasso from Wyoming and Senator Mike Lee from Utah, motivated by the belief that the Endangered Species Act is bad for business – for the fossil fuel industry and for some ranchers in rural areas – have been determined to introduce legislation that will fundamentally weaken the ESA. They are also minimizing the role of science, making it much more difficult to offer protection to endangered and threatened species.

Roughly sixteen hundred plants and animals have been listed on the endangered species list, with petitions for the addition of new species yearly by scientists and conservation groups, alongside those species being considered for delisting. It is a highly political process dependent on who holds the power in Congress.

'The Republicans are pushing bills to divert protection funding, prioritize corporate land development, and sidestep science,' says Representative Raul Grijalva, a Democrat from Arizona. 'These are blatant efforts to place corporate interests over species survival.' In fact, since 2017, more than twenty-five bills have been sponsored by Republicans to 'skirt, defang, weaken or undermine' the Endangered Species Act, says the National Resources Defense Council.

It is important to remember that America was the first country in the world to condemn human-caused extinction of other species and deem it illegal. John

Dingell, one of the authors of the Endangered Species Act in 1973, said: 'Protecting this Nation's wildlife and our public lands should never be a partisan or political issue; it should be about common sense . . . Living wild species are like a library of books still unread. Our heedless destruction of them is akin to burning that library without ever having read its books.'

Every species on the endangered register has its own beautiful, threatened story.

The gray wolf was listed as an endangered species in 1974, having been shot, poisoned, and trapped to near extinction. In 1995, wolves were reintroduced to central Idaho and Yellowstone National Park from Canada. Thirteen years later given their success, the gray wolf was delisted by the federal government. In the American West, controversy follows the wolf as surely as its howl calls up the moon. A lawsuit was filed immediately by Earth Justice on behalf of twelve conservation groups, challenging the decision to delist the gray wolf in the Northern Rockies. In July 2008, a federal court reinstated federal protections under the Endangered Species Act just in time to stop wolf hunting that had been implemented in Idaho, Montana, and Wyoming. This delisting and relisting dance in the courts around wolves continues seesawing between the politics and policies of each administration. Finally, on December 17, 2013, during a public comment period, roughly one million American citizens stood up and called for the protection of the gray wolf. It was one of the largest outcries on behalf of any species.

But old myths die hard, especially when it comes to wolves. Etched deep into our psyches are tales we heard as children that the wolf is the devil's dog dressed up like our grandmothers. Descriptions like 'bloodthirsty, vicious killers' are commonplace in some western towns. And on occasion, wolves kill sheep. This doesn't help their reputation.

On March 7, 2017, the Washington, D.C., Circuit Court of Appeals stripped Endangered Species Act protections from wolves in Wyoming. The panel of three judges issued a ruling in *Defenders of Wildlife, et al. v. Zinke, et al.*, reversing a district court decision that had restored protections for the Wyoming wolves. These legal battles are far from over, yet the story of the gray wolf returning to the American West remains an uplifting one – the story of a threatened species' recovery through impassioned individuals working with the science and conservation communities with vigilance, creativity, and care.

And then there is the Utah prairie dog. It is no secret how much I love them. Call them America's meerkats; they are a keystone species that creates habitat through elaborate tunneled towns that traditionally stretched for miles, offering more than two hundred species, from rattlesnakes to burrowing owls to black widows, a home. They are also a vital food source for raptors, coyotes, foxes, and badgers. These communal creatures declined to perilous numbers due to the politics of livestock that continues to claim prairie dog burrows are hazardous and can break the legs of horses and cattle. An aggressive poison campaign in the 1960s and '70s, alongside indiscriminate long-range target shooting, plague, and drought, has almost done them in. In 1972, fewer than two thousand Utah prairie dogs remained. They appeared on the original roster of protected species on the 1973 endangered species list. Names like 'popguts' and 'varmints' still follow them into their burrows. My own family must be responsible for killing hundreds of them. As a child, I became a devoted advocate of prairie dogs because I saw so many of them slaughtered as they ran between clumps of sagebrush fleeing from my brothers' shotguns. In college, I lobbied the Utah State Legislature on their behalf. Instead of lending their support, these largely male lawmakers handed me their wives' recipes for prairie dog stew.

In 2000, *The New York Times Magazine* listed the Utah prairie dog as one of the ten species least likely to survive the next hundred years. My heart broke. I wasn't alone. Such organizations as Wild Earth Guardians,

Defenders of Wildlife, and the Center for Biological Diversity led successful campaigns to educate the public on the plight of prairie dogs and took the federal government to court for their lack of protection. In 2013, the tide turned in favor of Utah prairie dogs when the Utah Nature Conservancy bought eight hundred acres through what is known as the School Institutional Trust Lands Administration (SITLA); lands that belong to the state can be sold with proceeds benefiting Utah schoolchildren. A Utah prairie dog sanctuary in Garfield County near Bryce Canyon National Park was created.

Today, the Utah prairie dog population is close to twenty thousand individuals, still less than 15 percent of its historic numbers, but we have the Endangered Species Act to thank for saving these wondrous creatures. Education matters and breaks down prejudices. In some instances, Utah prairie dog habitat is now being restored by the very ranchers who opposed them decades earlier. Financial incentives like paying ranchers to restore some of their private property for prairie dog habitat has helped. And the law has upheld their right to a dignified life.

Even so, the fate of prairie dogs – like wolves – is still marked by frontier thinking. In 2018, the US Supreme Court declined to hear an appeal from a group called People for the Ethical Treatment of

Property Owners of Cedar City, from a small rural community in Utah, that has challenged endangered species protections for Utah prairie dogs for decades, insisting they are overrun by these rodents. In a film made by the group, a particularly sinister scene showed a prairie dog stealing flowers from the grave of a newly buried resident, implying that this patriarch's death was brought on by the stress that prairie dogs caused him. The soundtrack was straight out of a horror movie. The Trump administration has been sympathetic to this cause and is moving to loosen the rules that have prevented people from shooting, poisoning, or transporting prairie dogs to other locations. My faith and solidarity remain with the Utah prairie dogs. They stand outside their burrows as small beacons of hope.

The 1973 Endangered Species Act has been more than 99 percent successful at preventing the extinction of species under its watch. Scientists credit the ESA for saving 227 species from going extinct.

To honor, uphold, and anticipate celebrating the anniversary of this noble decree into its centennial year in 2073, it is worth remembering that on December 28, 1973, when Congress passed the Endangered Species Act into law, it was truly a bipartisan bill. The vote in the Senate was 92 in favor, 0 opposed; in the House, it was 355 to 4. This seems miraculous, bordering on the impossible, given the rancor in Congress today.

President Richard M. Nixon spoke these words when he signed the Endangered Species Act into law:

Nothing is more priceless and more worthy of preservation than the rich array of animal life with which our country has been blessed. It is a many-faceted treasure, of value to scholars, scientists, and nature lovers alike, and it forms a vital part of the heritage we all share as Americans.

A journalist from Washington, D.C., recently asked me, 'Who is the most powerful individual in the American West right now?'

'Sage grouse,' I answered.

'I'm serious,' he said.

'So am I,' I replied.

In the Interior West, where sagebrush covers the landscape like a sea-blue haze, sage grouse are controlling the conversation around oil and gas development. The Bureau of Land Management projections show that nearly ninety-six thousand new oil and gas wells will be drilled over the next twenty years in six states: Colorado, Montana, North Dakota, South Dakota, Utah, and Wyoming. Oil wells could fragment 11.8 million acres of sagebrush and grassland habitat, an area larger than the state of New Hampshire.

Development, as planned, could affect the greater sage grouse populations by 19 percent.

Historic populations of sage grouse once numbered sixteen million, as they were part of the prairie ecosystem that included millions of bison and prairie dogs and pronghorns. Today, the population may be less than half a million, with many local populations in the vicinity of oil fields being drawn down to extinction.

One male sage grouse standing his ground on his ancestral lek against Shell Oil is akin to the lone man in China facing down a tank in Tiananmen Square.

Sage grouse are the latest bellwether species sounding the call for restraint on America's public lands. The bird was a 'candidate' for listing in 2015, and amendments were madly written by every western state, including Utah, which recognizes the economic stranglehold this bird could have on the future of fossil fuel development. States were highly motivated to come up with a reasonable plan that could manage the sage grouse outside of the perceived constraints of the Endangered Species Act.

On September 22, 2016, Sally Jewell, secretary of the interior during the Obama administration, signed a historic document on behalf of the greater sage grouse, stating that 'the charismatic rangeland bird . . . does not need to be protected under the Endangered Species

Act,' maintaining that through 'strong Federal, state, and private collaborations . . . we can successfully conserve landscapes and save species while providing certainty to rural communities.'

It was a bold compromise, with conservationists such as myself skeptical – but looking back, I admire Jewell's belief and her commitment to the process. The Fish and Wildlife Service worked with more than eleven hundred ranchers in eleven western states, with strong bipartisan leadership from the governors of Colorado, Wyoming, and Montana. Ninety-eight natural resource management plans detailing how various communities and states would protect grouse habitat were completed in collaboration with scientists, ranchers, conservationists, and local politicians. In the end, seventy million acres of public and private western rangeland were placed under protection.

Not surprisingly, two years later, this historic conservation initiative was largely undone by Sally Jewell's successor, Ryan Zinke. Secretary Zinke called for a review of the Sage Grouse Management Plans. *The New York Times* reported that the Bureau of Land Management 'intends to consider amending all or some of the land use plans finalized under the Obama Administration.' It was another sleight-of-hand move on behalf of the oil and gas industry.

On December 6, 2018, newspaper headlines across

the country read 'Zinke Moves to Weaken Landmark Greater Sage Grouse Conservation Plan.' It was his last act as secretary of the interior, 'a fine feather in his cap,' his defenders said.

Nine days later, on December 15, 2018, Ryan Zinke submitted his letter of resignation as secretary of the interior to President Trump, citing 'vicious and politically motivated attacks' on his character. In truth, the White House pressured him to do so. He left under a cloud of questions surrounding allegations of corruption and conflict of interest, some of which were reported to be the subject of Department of Justice investigations. David Bernhardt, a former lobbyist for the oil and gas industry, has taken Zinke's place as secretary of the interior. One month after his appointment, the Bureau of Land Management began auctioning 758,198 acres of public land for new oil and gas leases, including thirty-one parcels in Wyoming that biologists spoke out against with great urgency, saying that these lands up for bid contain 'the highest sage grouse density on Earth.' The sage grouse will now resume its power in the courts as national conservation groups petition the US Fish and Wildlife Service for the iconic bird to be listed as an endangered species.

It is not simply the future of the sage grouse that is imperiled by America's drive for oil independence, it is the entire sagebrush steppe ecosystem. For someone like me, who grew up in the Interior West where sagebrush was as ubiquitous as wind, the thought that this landscape, with its resident grouse, pronghorn, black-footed ferrets, and prairie dogs, would be threatened is unfathomable. It was not just common, it was our 'sagebrush ocean,' which stretched from the badlands of the Dakotas to the high plains and plateaus of Montana, Wyoming, and Idaho to the Great Basin playas of Nevada to the pinyon–juniper grasslands and red rock deserts of Utah, New Mexico, southern Colorado, and Arizona. Sage flats exist in California, as well.

This is the totemic power of the sage grouse, who joins the ranks of other species who have changed the course of public policy, local power structures, and the landscape itself, within western towns and cities. Consider the spotted owl and the salmon in the Pacific Northwest, which saved millions of acres of ancient forests from being felled. Add the gray wolf and the grizzly as species now defining the Greater Yellowstone Ecosystem. The mountain bluebird showed us the cascading effects of DDT; the black-footed ferret and its relationship to prairie dogs illuminated its role in vibrant grasslands; and the willow flycatcher and the woundfin minnow are measures of the health of the Colorado River. And there are so many more – from the Everglade kite to the monarch butterfly to the Preble's meadow jumping mouse, to hundreds of plants and creatures who are having a profound impact on how we understand what is integral to the integrity of natural ecosystems.

The beauty of the Endangered Species Act is that it is a federal act of empathy, put into writing and upheld by law. It is an enlightened act of mind and heart that is both visionary and inclusive. It proceeds from our Declaration of Independence and portends a Declaration of Interdependence. It gives us an opportunity to exercise our conscience and consciousness on behalf of all species.

The great consequence of the Endangered Species Act, over time, is that it ensures that we, as a species, will not be alone. We will remain part of a living, breathing, thriving community of vibrant beings with feathers, fins, and fur; roots, petals, and spines; trunks, branches, and leaves. It promises that creatures that walk with four legs or scurry on six or crawl with eight will move alongside upright *Homo sapiens* – our humanity walking side by side with our humility. Wild beauty sustains us. A wolverine becomes more than a thought; it makes each of us an heir to wonder.

The plants and animals are asking us for respect and restraint. The Endangered Species Act, designed in the late twentieth century, promises them that we will try. When my friend from Washington, D.C., asks me again about where power resides in the American West, I will ask him to accompany me in the spring to smell the sweet fragrance of sage after rain. And in that moment of reverie, just maybe we will hear the drumbeats of sage grouse rising above the oil rigs on the horizon.

The Endangered Species Act has never been more relevant and never been more at risk. As a conscious and conscientious citizenry, may we rededicate ourselves to its survival, especially as we face the future with climate change. Congress will need our support. So will the plants and animals.

We must be creative. We must be collaborative. And we must exercise our compassion on behalf of all species. Empathy moves us to action.

When I was writing the book *Finding Beauty in a Broken World*, I made the decision to link the plight of Utah prairie dogs with the Rwandan genocide. It was met with harsh criticism from human rights activists and literary critics. 'You cannot compare a rodent to a human being,' one individual said. But I would argue that they missed the point. The loss of a species and the loss of a people are both predicated on the same qualities of prejudice, cruelty, arrogance, and ignorance, ultimately creating the seedbed of war. We need a new conscience and consciousness in our relationship with the Other. And this has everything to do with cultivating peace.

The Endangered Species Act is both a policy and a prayer, in both forms calling out what Albert Schweitzer called the three most important words we can embrace: 'Reverence for life.'

Last month, I was invited to meet a lynx held in captivity while it was healing from a broken leg at a wildlife rehabilitation center in Idaho. I have never seen a lynx in the wild, but on that day, our eyes locked and I could not walk away. Finally, my name was being called. The people I came with were leaving. I left the lynx and then, at the last minute, I told my friends I had forgotten something. In truth, I needed more time with the lynx. I returned. Our eyes met again, neither of us blinked – something passed between us – and then, the lynx began to nod her head.

I will never know what this gesture implied, nor what the lynx was actually thinking. But for the rest of my life, I will remember her – believing that the animals among us are nodding their heads, waiting for us to respond to this moment in time. We are all endangered species on an endangered planet.

What is required of us is love. The Endangered Species Act is an act of love.

2019

The Erotic Landscape

To whom do I pray? A Spanish woman sits in the row across from me in the Iglesia de Santa Teresa, reciting her prayers in whispers as she rotates each bead of her rosary through her fingers. Her hands are folded beneath her chin. She alternates her prayers with the reading of scriptures.

To whom do I pray? I kneel before the statue of Santa Teresa, gilded and animated by the soft light in this small dark alcove. Her right hand is outstretched as though she were about to touch Spirit, her left hand covers her heart.

I close my eyes and listen.

After many minutes of silence, what comes into my mind unannounced is the phrase *'wet not dry.'*

I close my eyes tighter and concentrate more deeply, let these words simply pass through as one does with distractions in meditation. Again, I hear the words *'wet not dry.'* The woman across the aisle from me is weeping. Her private utterings, *'para ti, para ti,'* for you, for you, are audible. I open my eyes feeling little emotion and look down at the worn tiles beneath my feet. The Spanish woman faces the saint, bows, crosses herself, and leaves.

Wondering if I should be here at all, I try once again to pray. In stillness, the phrase returns to me.

All I can hear in the sanctity of this chapel is what sounds at best like a cheap antiperspirant jingle. I do not feel my heart. Am I numb to these things of the Spirit? Even the white gladiolus arranged as offerings appear as the bleached vertebrae of deer. Filled with shame, I look up at Santa Teresa's face.

Later that afternoon, I steady myself by sitting beneath an old cottonwood tree, similar to the ones I have sat under a hundred times in the desert. I open Santa Teresa's autobiography, *The Life of Saint Teresa of Ávila by Herself*: . . . *and God converted the dryness of my soul into a great tenderness.*

I turn another page: *Only once in my life do I remember asking Him for consolation and that was when I was very dry.* . . .

And another: *It is my opinion that though a soul may seem to be deriving some immediate benefit when it does anything to further itself in this prayer of union, it will in fact very quickly fall again, like buildings without foundations.* . . . *Remain calm in times of dryness.*

Santa Teresa's book articulates 'the Four Waters of

Prayer.' She says simply that wetness brings us 'to a recollected state.' A well. A spring. A fountain. To drink deeply from the Spirit and quench the aridity of the soul is to retrieve, revive, and renew our relationship with God.

Where are my tears? Where is the rain? I ask myself. *I am now speaking of that rain that comes down abundantly from heaven to soak and saturate the whole garden.*

The leaves of the cottonwood tree shield me from the heat as I read her *Confessions* slowly:

> *Who is this whom all my faculties thus obey? Who is it that in a moment sheds light amidst such great darkness, who softens a heart that seemed to be of stone and sheds the water of gentle tears where for so long it had seemed to be dry? Who gives these desires? Who gives this courage? What have I been thinking of? What am I afraid of?*

The smells of lavender and rosemary collide in the garden. Something breaks open in me. My soul is brittle, my body a desert. I weep. What might it mean to honor thirst before hunger and joy before obligation?

There is an image of a woman in the desert, her back arched as her hands lift her body up from black rocks. Naked. She spreads her legs over a boulder etched by the Ancient Ones; a line of white lightning zigzags from her mons pubis. She is perfectly in place, engaged, ecstatic, and wild. This is Judy Dater's photograph 'Self-Portrait with Petroglyphs.'

To be in relation to everything around us, above us, below us, earth, sky, bones, blood, flesh, is to see the world whole, even holy.

Another woman stands on her tiptoes, naked, holding draped fabric close to her body as it cascades over her breasts, down her belly and legs, like water. A strand of pearls hangs down her back; her eyes are closed.

This photograph, taken at Studio d'Ora in Vienna in 1934, is the first image I see in Det Erotiske Museum in Copenhagen, Denmark. I take another step into the foyer and find myself confronted with a six-foot golden phallus mounted on a pedestal. I am tempted to touch it, as I recall the bronze statues of women in museums around the world whose breasts and buttocks have been polished perfectly by the hands of men, but I refrain.

A visitor to this museum in Copenhagen can wander through four floors of exhibits ranging from a solitary Greek vase, circa 530 B.C., depicting Pan chasing Echo, to a wax tableau of Fanny Hill, 1749, to a prostitute's room reconstructed from an 1839 Danish police report.

Spiraling up to the fourth floor (you may choose to descend at this point to the Aphrodite Café for coffee and pastries), the visitor arrives at the Erotic Tabernacle, the climax of this museum experience. Here, you are assaulted with twelve television screens, four across and three down, which together create a montage of pornography from 1929 through 1990, complete with the music of Pink Floyd's 'The Wall.'

As I watch these images of men and women simultaneously moving from one position to the next, I wonder about our notion of the erotic – why it is so often aligned with the pornographic, the limited view of the voyeur watching the act of intercourse without any interest in the relationship itself.

I wonder what walls we have constructed to keep our true erotic nature tamed. And I am curious why we continue to distance ourselves from natural sources.

What are we afraid of?

The world we frequently surrender to defies our participation in nature and seduces us into believing that our only place in the wild is as spectator, onlooker. A society of individuals who only observe a landscape from behind the lens of a camera or the window of an automobile without entering in is perhaps no different from the person who obtains sexual gratification from looking at the sexual play of others.

The golden phallus I did not touch, in the end, did not touch me. It became a stump, a severance of the body I could not feel.

Eroticism, being in relation, calls the inner life into play. No longer numb, we feel the magnetic pull in our bodies toward something stronger, more vital than simply ourselves. Arousal becomes a dance with longing. We form a secret partnership with possibility.

I recall a day in the slickrock country of southern Utah where I was camped inside a small canyon outside Kanab. Before dawn, coyotes yipped, yapped, and sang. It was a chorus of young desert dogs.

The sun rose. There is a silence to creation. I stood and faced east, stretched upward, stretched down, pressed my hands together.

I knelt on the sand still marked by the patter of rain and lit my stove, which purred like my cat at home. I boiled water for tea, slowly poured it in my earthen cup, then dipped the rose hip tea bag in and out until the water turned pink. My morning ritual was complete as I wrapped my hands around the warmth of the cup and drank.

Not far, an old juniper stood in the clearing, deeply rooted and gnarled. I had never seen such a knowledgeable tree. Perhaps it was the silver sheen of its shredded bark that reminded me of my grandmother, her windblown hair in the desert, her weathered face, the way she held me as a child. I wanted to climb into the arms of this tree.

With both hands on one of its strongest boughs, I pulled myself up and lifted my right leg over the branch so I was straddling it. Leaning back into the body of the juniper, I brought my knees up to my chest and nestled in – hidden, perfectly shaded from the heat. I had forgotten what it felt like to really be held.

Hours passed, who knows how long; the angle of light shifted. Something had passed between us, evident by the change in my own countenance, the slowing of my pulse, and the softness of my eyes as though I was awakening from a desert trance.

I finally inched my way down, wrapping my hands around the trunk. Feet on Earth. I took out my water bottle and saturated the roots. Pink sand turned red. I left the desert in a state of wetness.

'The erotic has often been misnamed by men and used against women,' says Audre Lord in *Uses of the Erotic*.

It has been made into the confused, the trivial, the psychotic, and plasticized sensation. For this reason, we have turned away from exploration and consideration of the erotic as a source of power and information, confusing it with the pornographic. But pornography is a direct denial of the power of the erotic, for it represents the suppression of true feeling. Pornography emphasizes sensation without feeling.

Without feeling. Perhaps these two words are the key, the only way we can begin to understand our abuse of each other and our abuse of the land. Could it be that what we fear most is our capacity to feel, and so we annihilate symbolically and physically that which is beautiful and tender, anything that dares us to consider our creative selves? The erotic world is silenced, reduced to a collection of objects we can curate and control, be it a vase, a woman, or wilderness. Our lives become a piece in the puzzle of pornography as we go through the motions of daily intercourse without any engagement of the soul.

A group of friends gather in the desert – call it a pilgrimage – at the confluence of the Little Colorado and the Colorado Rivers in the Grand Canyon. It is high noon in June, hot, very hot. They walk upstream, men and women, moving against the current of the turquoise water. Nothing but deep joy can be imagined. Their arms fan the air as they teeter on unstable stones, white stones in the river. They are searching for mud the consistency of mousse and find it, delicious, milk chocolate mud, perfect for bathing. They take off their clothes and sink to their waists, turn, roll over, and wallow in pleasure. Their skins are slippery with clay. They rub each other's bodies; arms, shoulders, backs, torsos, even their faces are painted in mud, and they become the animals they are. Blue eyes. Green eyes. Brown eyes behind masks. In the heat, lying on ledges, they bake until they crack like terracotta. For hours, they dream the life of lizards.

In time, they submerge themselves in the Little Colorado, diving and surfacing freshly human.

D. H. Lawrence writes: 'There exist two great modes of life – the religious and the sexual.' Eroticism is the bridge.

The Erotic Museum in Copenhagen opened July 26, 1992. It closed August 31, 1993, because of financial difficulties. More than 100,000 visitors from around the world had paid to see erotica on display.

Standing on the sidewalk next to the red banners that advertise the museum, I watched each object, each exhibit, each wax figure, being carried out of the white building and loaded into two Volvo moving vans on Vesterbrogade 31, minutes away from Tivoli Gardens, where harlequins danced.

That was Labor Day weekend, 1993. Seven months later, the museum opened once again. The vision of Ole Ege, the founder of the Erotic Museum, is being celebrated once again, this time in a new location and with a more solid base of support.

'Denmark has been liberated sexually for twenty-five years,' he says. 'But we are not yet liberated in our minds. It is a matter of individual morality how one conceives this subject. For me, eroticism relates to all the highest and finest things of life. Every couple on Earth participates in this confirmation of creation, the urge we have to share ourselves, to make each other whole.'

The idea that governs an erotic museum and the ideal behind an erotic life may never find a perfect resolution. Here lies our dilemma as human beings: Nothing exists in isolation. We need a context for eros, not a pedestal, not a video screen. The lightning we witness crack and charge a night sky in the desert is the same electricity we feel in ourselves whenever we dare to touch flesh, rock, body, Earth. We must take our love outdoors where reciprocity replaces voyeurism, respect replaces indulgence. We can choose to photograph a tree or we can sit in its arms, where we are participating in wild nature, even our own.

The woman in the desert stands and extends her arms.

She speaks: *'Let the beauty of what we love be what we do. There are hundreds of ways to kneel and kiss the ground.' (Rumi)*

Ground Truthing

Ground Truthing: The use of a ground survey to confirm findings of aerial image or to calibrate quantitative aerial observations; validation and verification techniques used on the ground to support maps; walking the ground to see for oneself if what has been told is true; near-surface discoveries.

The Arctic is balancing on an immense mirror. The water table is visible. Pools of light gather: lakes, ponds, wetlands. The tundra is shimmering. One squints perpetually.

Drinking from the river – I am drinking from the river – this tincture of glaciers, this press of ice warmed by the sun. My arid heart has been waiting for decades, maybe three, for the return of this childhood pleasure of drinking directly from the source.

When my father asks me what it was like to visit the Arctic national Wildlife Refuge, I will simply say, 'We drank from the river.'

Experience opens us, creates a chasm in our heart, an expansion in our lungs, allowing us to pull in fresh air to all that was stagnant. We breathe deeply and remember fear for what it is – a resistance to the unknown.

It is a day of walking. Most decide to climb an unnamed peak. Cindy Shogan and I choose a more modest hike where we can find a vantage point to watch animals. To our great surprise, our attention focuses not on big mammals, but poppies.

We are on our bellies for a ground squirrel's look. Tissuelike petals form a yellow cup that literally holds light which translates to heat as the flowers turn their heads to continuously follow the sun. The blossom is supported on a threadlike stem. The poppies we meet have survived the pounding rains and brutal winds of the past three days. Not a petal is torn or tattered. They simply raise their heads toward the sun and lure in flies with the seduction of warmth.

Cindy, the executive director of the Alaska Wilderness League, is one of the smartest strategists of her generation. She talks about the political challenges presented by the Bush administration and their relentless drive to drill for oil in the Arctic National Wildlife Refuge.

I ask her what she fears most. Ever the optimist, Cindy says, 'We're not going to lose the Arctic, it's just the opposition's endless bombardment and trickery.'

Alaska's senior senator, Ted Stevens, head of the powerful Appropriations Committee, is now planning to attach his drilling proposal to any piece of legislation that can be brought, from energy to transportation.

This is Cindy's first trip to the refuge. We are here to see the lands left in limbo, coldly referred to in Washington as 'the 1002' (ten-o-two), a number referring to a particular amendment which says that these 1.2 million acres within the Arctic National Wildlife Refuge could be opened for oil and gas development. These disputed lands are part of the Coastal Plain, where the great caribou migrations occur – the long sweep of land that stretches from the foothills of the Brooks Range to the Beaufort Sea.

Cindy and I discuss the story of Subhankar Banerjee, a talented young photographer from India who quit his job, cashed in his savings in 2000, and has been taking pictures of the Arctic ever since. He recently published a book titled *Arctic National Wildlife Refuge: Seasons of Life and Land.*

In March 2003, during the budget debate, US Senator Barbara Boxer introduced an amendment to prevent consideration of drilling in the refuge from being added to the bill. She held Banerjee's book up on the Senate floor as an example of the elegance of this place and why it deserves protection. She then invited members to visit Mr Banerjee's upcoming show at the Smithsonian Institution. Ted Stevens took note and said, 'People who vote against this today are voting against me, and I will not forget it.' Boxer's amendment passed anyway.

A few weeks later, the show Subhankar Banerjee had been promised by the Smithsonian, which was to hang in a central location near the rotunda, had suddenly been relegated to the basement. Evocative captions offering a rationale for conservation with quotations by Peter Matthiessen, David Allen Sibley, Jimmy Carter, and others had been removed and replaced with perfunctory labels such as 'Buff-breasted Sandpiper: Coastal plain of the Jago River.' A cry of foul play went out in Washington and in May 2003, Senator Richard Durbin used a hearing on the Smithsonian's budget to question whether outside influence had been used to move Subhankar's exhibition.

It was Cindy and the Alaska Wilderness League that placed a copy of Subhankar Banerjee's book in Senator Boxer's hands. It was also Cindy who nudged Senator Durbin for an investigation. She did not tell me these facts. I had to find these details in the press.

Subhankar Banerjee has become, unwittingly, a celebrity photographer who bears the distinction of being censored by the United States government. For what? The threat of beauty.

In the open space of democracy, beauty is not optional, but essential to our survival as a species.

In a few days, we will reach the confluence of the Marsh Fork and the Canning River. The Canning is the fluid western boundary of the Arctic National Wildlife Refuge that determines where one can now drill and where one cannot. It will carry us into the heart of this national debate. Right now, the rallying cry and corruption of politics seem a world apart from the world we are in, because in the rock-hard, ice-sculpted reality of the Arctic – they are.

Arctic still life: a caribou antler, laced with lichen, orange and yellow, is wrapped around a dwarf willow which now provides shade and shelter for what was once held high in motion.

Cindy finds a piece of qiviut, musk ox hair, and hands it to me.

What will we make of the life before us? How do we translate the gifts of solitary beauty into the action required for true participatory citizenship?

Brooks Yeager, Cindy's husband, has just come down the mountain. He was assistant secretary for policy in the Department of the Interior during the Clinton administration, when he labored long and hard on behalf of the Arctic. He has tender eyes and this trip for him, as it is for all of us, is a 'ground truth-ing' to see if what he has fought for and imagined is true. He knows firsthand how politics translates into policy and how much is bargained away in bills before Congress.

More rain. More stories. They pop open like umbrellas. Jim Campbell, our guide, tall and lean, with gray, cropped hair and large, skilled hands, crouches down over the stove to make coffee. He knows wilderness intimately, the wilderness of war and the wilderness of peace. For more than twenty years, he has traversed the Brooks Range by foot, run its rivers, and camped night after night in the buoyancy of the tundra.

He tells of coming home from Vietnam in 1968, walking into his father's tavern in Pennsylvania, still in uniform, completely disoriented. A few weeks later, he found himself holding the security line in Chicago at the Democratic Convention and fighting the antiwar protesters. 'Nothing made sense,' he says. 'Nothing.' And then, just a year or so ago, he attended a ceremony for Vietnam veterans in Fairbanks, Alaska. 'Welcome home,' a woman said to him. Jim paused, holding back emotion. 'It was the first time I had heard those words.'

Light shifts. An opening is created. We step outside the cook tent and place four topographical maps that encompass the 19.5 million acres of the Arctic National Wildlife Refuge on the ground to see where we are and where we are going. We will cover another ten to fifteen miles on the river today. In a week, we will be camping on the Coastal Plain.

Scale cannot be registered here in human terms. It is geologic, tectonic, and planetary. Stegosaurus-like ridgelines form the boundaries of our passage. Ribbon-like waterfalls cascade for miles down cliffs. What I thought was a swallow became an eagle. Weather changes minute by minute. Gray tumultuous clouds weave themselves into patterns of herringbone, yet a strange softness abides, even in the razor-cut terror of this rugged terrain.

Coming into the confluence where the Marsh Fork meets the Canning River feels celebratory. It is a great flooding, far and wide. Blinding light ricochets off platinum strands of water. Braided rivers, braided energies. Wild waters intertwine. We pull the boat over a few rock gardens until we find the deeper channels. The roots of silver-leafed willows, exposed in the cut bank, tremble like the nervous system of the Arctic.

I cannot sleep and slip from the comfort of our tent to face the low, diffused glow of midnight. All colors bow to the gentle arc of light the sun creates as it strolls across the horizon. Green steppes become emerald. The river, lapis. A patch of cotton grass ignites. My eyes catch the illumined wings of a tern, an Arctic tern, fluttering, foraging above the river – the embodiment of grace, suspended. The tern animates the vast indifference with its own vibrant intelligence. Black cap; blood-red beak pointed down; white body with black-tipped wings. With my eyes laid bare, I witness a bright thought in big country. While everyone is sleeping, the presence of this tern hovering above the river, alive, alert, engaged, becomes a vision of what is possible.

On this night, I met the Arctic Angel and vowed the 22,000 miles of her migratory path between the Arctic and Antarctica would not be in vain. I will remember her. No creature on Earth has spent more time in daylight than this species. No creature on Earth has shunned darkness in the same way as the Arctic tern. No creature carries the strength and delicacy of determination on its back like this slight bird. If air is the medium of the Spirit, then the Arctic tern is its messenger.

What I know is this: when one hungers for light it is only because one's knowledge of the dark is so deep.

A grizzly has just circled the rock. Tom Campion spotted him first from the river. We stop, tie down our boats, and hike to a knoll where we can watch from a safe distance, separated by a ravine. The grizzly is pawing the ground for roots. The bear is oblivious to us. We are not oblivious of the bear. We sit down and eat lunch, mindful of where and how the grizzly is moving. An upland sandpiper cries, circles us, and raises her wings as she lands. Light breaks through clouds and catches the bear's honey-colored coat, with a brown line traveling down his hump and back. His massive body, moving in all its undulating power, makes my blood quiver. I note his small eyes, his large head, and the length of his claws, perfect for digging. Another hour flies. We eat and watch as he eats and saunters. The wind shifts, the bear looks up, stands, and sniffs the air. We freeze. He turns and runs downhill.

It is called 'Bear Shaman' – an Iñupiat sculpture carved out of soapstone. At one end is Man, crouched close to the earth. At the other end is Bear, in search of prey. Both Man and Bear live inside the same body. Their shared heart determines who will be seen and who will disappear. Shape-shifting is its own form of survival.

For several days, we have been floating the Canning River. In the end, we will have covered almost 125 miles. We are now camped on the famed 1002 lands. On one side of the river is the Arctic National Wildlife Refuge. On the other side are the Alaska State lands where oil and gas exploration is underway. Keep walking west and you'll bump into Prudhoe Bay.

I thought I saw a musk ox across the river. It was an empty oil drum.

The Arctic is made up of dreams. And not everyone's is the same. My dream of the Arctic National Wildlife Refuge was planted in my heart by Mardy Murie. The year was 1974. The place was Moose, Wyoming, at the Murie Ranch where the famed naturalists, Olaus and Adolph, with their wives, Mardy and Louise, made their home at the base of the Tetons.

I was a student at the Teton Science School. I was eighteen years old. Mardy introduced us to Alaska through her stories of growing up in Fairbanks, of Olaus's field work studying caribou for the US Fish and Wildlife Service in 1920. She showed us her slides of their summer on the Sheenjek River in 1956 with Olaus, Brina Kessel, Bob Krear, and George Schaller. She shared with us their dream of Arctic protection, and the dedication of their group of friends, including Bob Marshall, Ed Zahnhiser, George Collins, Lowell Sumner, Starker Leopold, writers Sigurd Olson and Lois Crisler, and Supreme Court Justice William O. Douglas, along with local conservationists Celia Hunter and Ginny Wood, who helped build a state and national constituency for the creation of the Arctic National Wildlife Range, placing pressure on Congress until it was created in 1960.

Revolutionary patience. This community of Americans never let go of their wild, unruly faith that love can lead to social change. The Muries believed that the protection of wildlands was the protection of natural processes, the unseen presence in wilderness. The Wilderness Act, another one of their dreams, was signed in 1964.

It was Mardy who inspired me to join her and a thousand others on June 5, 1977, to attend the Alaska Lands Hearings in Denver, Colorado. I hitched a ride with friends; we slept on the floor of a church. The next morning, road weary, we cleaned ourselves up and found seats inside the capitol building. This was one of the many regional hearings conducted by the House Interior Subcommittee on General Oversight and Alaskan Lands.

Those who wanted to offer testimony signed up. Mardy was among the first to be called forward. I remember her white braided hair, her poise, her strength. Her love of Alaska transcended her words. When she stood before the presiding congressman, Representative John Seiberling, her whole history and community stood with her.

'I am testifying as an emotional woman,' I can still remember her saying, 'and I would like to ask you, gentlemen, what's wrong with emotion?'

Perhaps she was remembering the emotion in Olaus's

voice when he testified before the Senate two decades earlier and said:

> *We long for something more, something that has a mental, a spiritual impact on us. This idealism, more than anything else, will set us apart as a nation striving for something worthwhile in the universe. It is inevitable, if we are to progress as people in the highest sense, that we shall become ever more concerned with the saving of the intangible resources as embodied in this move to establish the Arctic Wildlife Range.*

I have held this dream of visiting the Arctic for thirty years. That the refuge has become a symbol for how we define our national priorities is a testament to its innate power. That it continues to survive, resist, and absorb our own greed and economic tensions, year after year, is evidence of the force of love that has protected these wildlands for generations.

As the Brooks Range recedes behind us, I am mindful that Mardy is approaching 101 years of age. She has never shed her optimism for wild Alaska. I am half her age and my niece, Abby, is half of mine. We share her passion for this order of quiet freedom. America's wildlands are vulnerable and they will always be assailable as long as what we value in this nation is measured in monetary terms, not spiritual ones.

What are we willing to give our lives to if not the perpetuation of the sacred? Can we continue to stand together in our collective wisdom and say, these particular lands are inviolable, deserving protection by law and the inalienable right of safe passage for all beings that dwell here? Wilderness designation is the promise of this hope held in trust.

The open space of democracy provides justice for all living things – plants, animals, rocks, and rivers, as well as human beings.

We are camped on Shublik Island, another part of the 1002 lands, what Cindy and Brooks call 'the soul of the Arctic.' Cindy has the maps out, looking at Red Hill and the miles we paddled yesterday on the river, close to twenty-five. It was a long, arduous day and our muscles ache.

A fragrance drifts across the Canning. Without thought, each of us begins breathing deeply. Sighs emerge on the exhale. We are being drugged by perfume. An innocence is wafting on the wind. I am weeping and I don't know why. Brooke stands up in our boat and points. The plains are magenta all the way to the horizon, a blanket of petals, pink and violet variations of wild sweet pea.

When I ask Carol Kasza to describe the Arctic National Wildlife Refuge in one word, she doesn't hesitate. 'Wholeness,' she says. I am in the back of the boat with her as she steers us ahead to our last camp.

'It's not just the refuge or ANWR, the 1002, the National Petroleum Reserve Area, or any of the other throwaway names that are being bantered about in Washington,' she explains, 'but the entire region of what lives and breathes in the shadow of the Brooks Range with all its peaks and valleys, braided rivers, and coastlines. It's this layered sense of wilderness, the uninterrupted vistas without man's hand on it.

'If we choose to continue to only focus on particular areas, then this whole region becomes part of an intellectual and political project of fragmentation. Do we have to keep cutting it up into smaller and smaller bits and pieces until we finally call it a compromise? The Arctic National Wildlife Refuge is already a compromise – it was in 1960 and again in 1980.'

Carol, a woman in her fifties, is as fierce and wise and beautiful as the lines that give her face expression. She is a woman who has made her work her passion and has brought her whole family into her explorer's heart.

'I want to hear a different discussion,' she says. 'I want people to ask, "How does it feel to be in this country? What do you remember here that you have otherwise forgotten? Why do we want to destroy or diminish anything that inspires us to live more honestly?" '

The sanctity of solitude: I sit above a lake after a long walk up the steppe and then north across the tundra. Two swans are mirrored in the water.

A long-tailed jaeger sits next to me. I try not to move. With my legs crossed and my eyes barely open, I enter the space of meditation.

A wolf howls. My body leaps. The jaeger flies. Fear floods my heart. Presence creates presence. I am now alert. To feel yourself prey is to be shocked back into the reality of the Arctic's here and now.

This is what I have learned in these short weeks in the refuge:

You cannot afford to make careless mistakes, like meditating in the presence of wolves, or topping your boots in the river, or losing a glove, or not securing your tent down properly. Death is a daily occurrence in the wild, not noticed, not respected, not mourned. In the Arctic, I've learned ego is as useless as money.

> *Choose one's traveling companions well. Physical strength and prudence are necessary. Imagination and ingenuity are our finest traits.*
> *Expect anything.*
> *You can change your mind like the weather.*
> *Patience is more powerful than anger. Humor is more attractive than fear.*

Pay attention. Listen. We are most alive when
*   discovering.*
Humility is the capacity to see.
Suffering comes, we do not have to create it.
We are meant to live simply.
We are meant to be joyful.
Life continues with and without us.
Beauty is another word for God.

Here is my question: what might a different kind of power look like, feel like? And can power be distributed equitably among ourselves, even beyond our own species?

The power of nature is the power of a life in association. Nothing stands alone. On my haunches, I see a sunburst lichen attached to limestone; algae and fungi are working together to break down rock into soil. I cannot help but recognize a radical form of democracy at play. Each organism is rooted in its own biological niche, drawing its power from its relationship to other organisms. An equality of being contributes to an ecological state of health and succession.

'We can only attain harmony and stability by consulting ensemble,' writes Walt Whitman. This is my definition of community, and community interaction is the white-hot center of a democracy that burns bright.

Within the refuge, if I rotate slowly in place, what I see is a circumference of continuity. What I feel is a spiritual cohesion born out of wholeness. It is organic, cellular. I am at home in the peace of an intact world. The open space of democracy is not interested in hierarchies but in networks and systems where power is circular, not linear; a power reserved not for an entitled few, but shared and maintained by many. Public lands are our public commons and they belong to everyone. We enter these sacred lands soulfully and remember what it is we have forgotten – the gift of time and space. The Arctic National Wildlife Refuge is the literal open space of democracy. The privilege of being here is met with the responsibility I feel to experience and express its compounding grace.

Raw, wild beauty is a deeply held American value. It is its own declaration of independence. Equality is experienced through humility. Liberty is expressed through the simple act of wandering.

3:00 a.m. Divine light. I am called out of the tent by the sun. I walk north, blinded by its radiance. On top of the ridge, I see two figures – human – Jim and Kyle. I wave. They wave back. Kyle raises his arms above his head with bent elbows. I understand. Caribou. I walk briskly up toward the men.

'Thousands upon thousands of caribou,' Jim says. I turn. My binoculars scan the landscape for several minutes. Heads, antlers, backs, tails, legs, hooves, one caribou merges into another. Calves are jumping next to their mothers. It is an endless stream of animals walking across the tundra. Without field glasses, they register as a heat wave. I cannot take my eyes off them.

Jim and Kyle walk down to the flats and wake everyone. One by one, they rise from their tents. They rise to a rainbow, and another. A double rainbow is arching over the plains in Arctic light and we watch, as human beings have always watched, the great herds in motion.

2004

Engagement

It is unusually still. I am standing in Mardy and Olaus Murie's living room in Moose, Wyoming. It is the first time I have entered their home since Mardy passed away on October 19, 2003. She was 101 years old.

My eyes travel around the cabin. A Presidential Medal of Freedom is perched on the mantle of their stone fireplace. On the far wall is a piece of calligraphy, the words Mardy spoke at the Jackson Hole High School commencement in 1974: 'Give yourself the adventure of doing what you can do, with what you have, even if you have nothing but the adventure of trying. How much better than standing in a corner with your back to the wall.'

I am standing in the corner with my back to the wall. Never have I felt such dismay over the leadership and public policies of our nation. Never have I felt such determination and faith in our ability to change our country's current direction. How to reconcile these seemingly contradictory emotions in an election year when we appear to be anything but united states?

Snow is banked against the windows, melting. Last night, there was a conversation between great gray owls on the ranch. I think of all the conversations that took place in the warmth of this log home in the middle of the Tetons; imagine the stories told, the secrets shared, and the strategies developed to safeguard wildlands in this country. I recall the cups of tea poured and the plates of cookies passed at my own visits and how I always left believing what was possible, never doubting what was not.

The Muries and their circle of friends challenged the ethical structure of the United States government and institutions such as the US Fish and Wildlife Service. Olaus and his brother, Adolph, changed the public's perception of predators through their research on coyotes in Yellowstone and wolves in Denali. Olaus supported his colleague Rachel Carson when she was under fire from the Department of Agriculture following the publication of *Silent Spring*. Mardy campaigned endlessly for the protection of wild Alaska; they changed laws and made new ones, even the Wilderness Act of 1964.

What I wish I could ask Mardy now is, how do we engage in the open space of democracy in times of terror?

I believe she would send me home.

★

Castle Valley is a small desert community in south-eastern Utah. Large cottonwood trees shadow the creeks that flow from the high country down through the juniper, piñon, and sage. The Colorado River creates its northern boundary; the LaSal Mountains rise to the south; Castleton Tower stands to the east, next to a geologic formation locals call 'The Priest and Nuns'; and Porcupine Rim runs due west. The town is surrounded by 9,000 acres of Utah School Institutional Trust Lands, the blue squares that appear on state maps across the American West like a checkerboard. These school trust lands were created at statehood by the US Congress with the understanding that they could be sold to generate income for education. And beyond the trust lands, three wilderness study areas frame the valley: Morning Glory, Mary Jane, and Fisher Towers. The valley now supports around three hundred residents. If you drive in for a visit you will be greeted by a sign that says, 'caution: falling sky.'

Brooke and I moved to Castle Valley from Salt Lake City in the fall of 1998. The silence was both welcome and unsettling. The wind was a constant reminder that this erosional landscape is still in motion. The only thing we found we could count on was changing weather – the extreme heat of summer and extreme cold in winter. Fall and spring were seasons aligned with heaven. The daily tides of deer became our cue to when we awoke and when we retired. Our neighbors were both warm and solitary. We all shared a love of quiet and a sense of community, within reason – people largely left each other alone.

In the spring of 1999, the Utah School Institutional Trust Lands Administration (SITLA) sold eighty acres at the base of Parriott Mesa at a public auction to a developer in Aspen with a partner in Moab, without proper notice to the community of Castle Valley. The developers assured the town that the land was bought for a dwelling for one of their daughters. But within a matter of weeks, a large for sale sign was placed on wooden stilts and hammered into the red desert, the price of the land tripling. Parriott Mesa was now slated for a subdivision.

Castle Valley is not an affluent community. Most incomes fall below the national average. There was concern about what a high-end development would do to taxes and everyone knew water was a serious issue, with the Castle Valley aquifer dropping due to drought. The community panicked, and within days a meeting was called. The small adobe home belonging to Susan Ulery was packed with people: Mormons, non-Mormons, Republicans, Democrats, Libertarians, attorneys, carpenters, climbers, artists, teachers, and old hippies – the full range was in attendance.

We recognized Castleton Tower as the flame of

America's Redrock Wilderness. We talked about how the ecological integrity of the Colorado River Corridor was at stake if the SITLA lands were to be developed; we acknowledged the hundreds of oil and gas leases that could be activated. We believed there had to be viable alternatives. Out of our shock, anger, and affection for each other, the Castle Rock Collaboration (CRC) was formed. We had no money. We had no power. We had only our shared love of home and a desire for dialogue with the open spaces that defined our town.

Meanwhile, under the cover of darkness, the large for sale sign disappeared – only to reappear the next morning beneath Turret Arch inside Arches National Park, complete with telephone number. Shortly after dawn, both the developer and the Park Service received calls from numerous tourists enthusiastically interested in purchasing the arch. The developer was delighted, having thought he had missed something spectacular at the base of Parriott Mesa. The park rangers were baffled until they took a drive and saw the sign for themselves. Photographs were taken. The point was made. These developers would sell anything if they could, even our national parks.

The story rocked Castle Valley. Panic was replaced by humor. Nobody knew who did it; Coyote had entered town. This is, after all, Abbey's Country.

A few weeks later we learned that the developers

were going to strip the land on Monday, May 24, 1999. But an anonymous donor came forward literally the day before the bulldozers were set to roll and wrote CRC a check. With the help of Utah Open Lands, we were able to make the developers an offer and buy back the eighty acres as our first act in the name of community trust.

Suddenly, the Castle Rock Collaboration was taken seriously.

Suddenly, we did not feel so powerless.

After arduous conversations, SITLA agreed not to auction off any new parcels of land until the planning process was complete. Together, we hired a planning firm from Boulder, Colorado, to help lay out a strategy for responsible land use. With the help of companies like Petzl, Patagonia, and Black Diamond, and through the support of The Access Fund, the Castle Rock Collaboration was able to raise the money necessary to purchase the wide sweep of land at the base of Castleton Tower.

In the five years that we have been engaged in this process with SITLA, the Castle Rock Collaboration and its partners have protected over three thousand acres and raised nearly four million dollars. But perhaps the most important outcome has been the creation of an atmosphere of engagement with other committed individuals who live along the Colorado

River Corridor. We are learning that a community engaged is a community empowered.

If we listen to the land, we will know what to do.

In the open space of democracy we are listening – ears alert – we are watching – eyes open – registering the patterns and possibilities for engagement. Some acts are private; some are public. Our oscillations between local, national, and global gestures map the full range of our movement. Our strength lies in our imagination, and paying attention to what sustains life, rather than what destroys it.

> *And I know that what is popularly called politics is only a tiny part of what causes history to move.*
>
> – *W.H. Auden*
> *The Prolific and the Devourer*

In the fall of 2002, I was living in Italy. There was a growing fear that America was going to wage war in Iraq. There was also a growing resistance throughout Europe to the militant Bush-Blair partnership. An estimated one million people gathered in Florence; they walked the streets of Firenze, creating a body politic seven kilometers long.

This news was not being reported in America.

I wrote a letter home in the form of an op-ed piece

for the *Salt Lake Tribune*. I wanted my community to know about this calm manifestation of willful resolve demonstrating a simple fact: Even if our political leaders cannot read the pulse of a changing world, the people do. The European Social Forum had just held its meetings in Florence, where issues ranging from health and the environment to international trade to the possibility of a war in Iraq were discussed. It ended with this gesture of movement, much of it along the banks of the Arno River, creating a river of another sort, a river of humans engaged in a diverse dialogue of peace.

Train after train stopped and emptied itself of the working middle class. Men, women, and children from Italian towns and villages gathered to participate with citizens from all over Europe. Massimo Sottani, a former mayor of Regello whom I had met in the village where I was staying, had invited me to join him with his family and friends. 'It is not only our right and obligation to participate in civic life, it is in our best interest,' he said as we stood outside the station waiting for more of his friends.

Lorenzo Becawtini, a businessman in Florence, joined us. 'Antiglobalization is not a slogan,' he said, 'it is a rigorous reconfiguration of democracy that places power and creativity back into the hands of villagers and townspeople, providing them with as many choices as possible.'

With antiglobalization in Europe often tied to anti-Americanism, there were the inevitable placards of George W. Bush disguised as Hitler next to banners that read 'Drop Bush not bombs' and a Big Mac being driven on top of a hearse. But for the most part, the focal point of this massive demonstration remained on positive changes for a changing world.

At one point, an elderly Florentine man who held memories of Mussolini stepped out on his balcony above the wave of people and draped a white bedsheet over the railing in support of peace. As participants waved to the old man, the crowd spontaneously began singing '*Ciao, Bella, Ciao,*' the song of the *partigianos*, the Italian resistance against the fascists in World War II. Neighbor after neighbor repeated the gesture, draping white sheets and pillow cases over their balconies until the apartment walls that lined the streets appeared as great sails billowing in the breeze.

Albertina Pisano, a twenty-five-year-old student from the University of Milan, said, 'My generation in Europe doesn't know what it means to be at war. I came to the forum to listen and participate.' When I asked her if she thought this would make any difference, she answered, 'It is making a difference to me.'

Looking over my shoulder from the rise on the bridge, all I could see was an endless river of people walking, many hand-in-hand, all side-by-side, peacefully, united in place with a will for social change. Michel-angelo was among them, as art students from Florence raised replicas of his *Prigioni* above their heads, the unfinished sculptures of prisoners trying to break free from the confines of stone. Machiavelli was among them, as philosophy students from Rome carried his words: 'There is nothing more difficult to take in hand, more perilous to conduct, or more uncertain in its success than to take the lead in the introduction of a new order of things.' Leonardo da Vinci was among them, his words carrying a particularly contemporary sting: 'And by reason of their boundless pride . . . there shall be nothing remaining on the earth or under the earth or in the waters that shall not be pursued and molested or destroyed.'

The hundreds of thousands of individuals who walked together in the name of social change could be seen as the dignified, radical center walking boldly toward the future. As an American in Florence, I won-dered, how do we walk with the rest of the world when our foreign policies seem to run counter to the rising global awareness of a world hungry for honest diplomacy?

As I look back over the story we have been living in Castle Valley, it does not begin to convey the power and empowering nature of the process. It is through the process of defining what we want as a town that we are becoming a real community. It is through the act of participation that we change.

This is not simply a story of not-in-my-backyard. It is the unfolding tale of how a small community in the desert is rising to its own defense, saying, we believe we have a stake in the future of our own community, which we choose to define beyond our own boundaries of time and space and species.

A crisis woke us up. A shared love of place opened a dialogue with neighbors. We asked for help. We found partners. We used our collective intelligence to formulate a plan. And then we had to search within ourselves to find what each of us had to give.

In my private moments of despair, I am aware of the limits of my own imagination. I am learning in Castle Valley that imaginations shared invite collaboration and collaboration creates community. A life in association, not a life independent, is the democratic ideal. We participate in the vitality of the struggle.

Social change takes time. Communities are built on the practice of patience and imagination – the belief that we are here for the duration and will take care of our relations in times of both drought and abundance. These are the blood and flesh gestures of commitment.

In thousands of local narratives being written around America, enlivened citizenship is activated each time we knock on our neighbors' doors, each time we sit down together and share a meal.

In our increasingly fundamentalist country, we have to remember what is fundamental: gravity – what draws us to a place and keeps us there, like love, like kinship. When we commit to a particular place, a certain element of choice is removed. We begin to see the world whole instead of fractured. Long-term strategies replace short-term gains. We inform one another and become an educated public that responds.

Here in the redrock desert, which now carries the weight of more leases for oil and gas than its fragile red skin can support, due to the aggressive energy policy of the Bush administration, the open space of democracy appears to be closing. The Rocky Mountain states are feeling this same press of energy extraction with scant thought being given to energy alternatives. A domestic imperialism has crept into our country with the same assured arrogance and ideology-of-might that seem evident in Iraq.

It is easy to believe we the people have no say; that the powers in Washington will roll over our local concerns with their corporate energy ties and thumper trucks. It is easy to believe that the American will is only focused on how to get rich, how to be entertained, and how to distract itself from the hard choices we have before us as a nation.

I refuse to believe this. The only space I see truly capable of being closed is not the land or our civil liberties but our own hearts.

The human heart is the first home of democracy. It is where we embrace our questions. Can we be equitable? Can we be generous? Can we listen with our whole beings, not just our minds, and offer our attention rather than our opinions? And do we have enough resolve in our hearts to act courageously, relentlessly, without giving up – ever – trusting our fellow citizens to join with us in our determined pursuit of a living democracy?

The heart is the house of empathy whose door opens when we receive the pain of others. This is where bravery lives, where we find our mettle to give and receive, to love and be loved, to stand in the center of uncertainty with strength, not fear, understanding this is all there is. The heart is the path to wisdom because it dares to be vulnerable in the presence of power. Our power lies in our love of our homelands.

The heart embodies faith because it leads us to charity. It is the muscle behind hope that brings confidence to those who despair.

Democracy depends on engagement, a firsthand

accounting of what one sees, what one feels, and what one thinks, followed by the artful practice of express-ing the truth of our times through our own talents, gifts, and vocations.

Question. Stand. Speak. Act.

We have a history of bravery in this nation and we must call it forward now. Our future is guaranteed only by the degree of our personal involvement and commitment to an inclusive justice.

In the open space of democracy, we engage the qualities of inquiry, intuition, and love as we become a dynamic citizenry, unafraid to exercise our shared knowledge and power. We can dissent. We can vote. We can step forward in times of terror with a con-founding calm that will shatter fear and complacency.

It is time to ask, when will our national culture of self-interest stop cutting the bonds of community to shore up individual gain and instead begin to nourish communal life through acts of giving, not taking? It is time to acknowledge the violence rendered to our souls each time a mountaintop is removed to expose a coal vein in Appalachia or when a wetland is drained, dredged, and filled for a strip mall. And the time has come to demand an end to the wholesale dismissal of the sacredness of life in all its variety and forms, as we witness the repeated breaking of laws, and the relaxing of laws, in the sole name of growth and greed.

We have made the mistake of confusing democracy with capitalism and have mistaken political engagement with a political machinery we all understand to be corrupt. It is time to resist the simplistic, utilitarian view that what is good for business is good for humanity in all its complex web of relationships. A spiritual democracy is inspired by our own sense of what we can accomplish together, honoring an integrated society where the social, intellectual, physical, and economic well-being of all is considered, not just the wealth and health of the corporate few.

'A patriot must always be ready to defend his country against his government,' said Edward Abbey. To not be engaged in the democratic process, to sit back and let others do the work for us, is to fall prey to bitterness and cynicism. It is the passivity of cynicism that has broken the back of our collective outrage. We succumb to our own depression believing there is nothing we can do.

I do not believe we can look for leadership beyond ourselves. I do not believe we can wait for someone or something to save us from our global predicaments and obligations. I need to look in the mirror and ask this of myself: If I am committed to seeing the direction of our country change, how must I change myself?

We are a people addicted to speed and superficiality, and a nation that prides itself on moral superiority. But our folly lies in not seeing what we base our superiority on. Wealth and freedom? What is wealth if we cannot share it? What is freedom if we cannot offer it as a vision of compassion and restraint, rather than force and aggression? Without an acknowledgement of complexity in a society of sound bites, we will not find the true source of our anger or an authentic passion that will propel us forward to the place of personal engagement.

We are in need of a reflective activism born out of humility, not arrogance. Reflection, with deep time spent in the consideration of others, opens the door to becoming a compassionate participant in the world.

'To care is neither conservative nor radical,' writes John Ralston Saul. 'It is a form of consciousness.' To be in the service of something beyond ourselves – to be in the presence of something other than ourselves, together – this is where we can begin to craft a meaningful life where personal isolation and despair disappear through the shared engagement of a vibrant citizenry.

2004

Wild Mercy

The eyes of the future are looking back at us and they are praying for us to see beyond our own time. They are kneeling with hands clasped that we might act with restraint, that we might leave room for the life that is destined to come. To protect what is wild is to protect what is gentle. Perhaps the wildness we fear is the pause between our own heartbeats, the silent space that says we live only by grace. Wilderness lives by this same grace.

Wild mercy is in our hands.